Praise for "An Autobiography"

An ambitious recounting of a life well-traveled, this poem began the day it's author was born. When the colors blue, red and yellow exploded him into the world he was offered to walk. So intent is his relationship with nature and its cycles - its calm and terrifying transformations - the reader rides with him as he creates ropes of words to hold on to. We hold on as he demands his right to play with the sea, with the moon, with the sun and with those recurring blue eyes. Are they his or do they belong to his love, his partner, his witness? Our protagonist, principal character of the life he shares with flowers and gods, constantly sees, questions, challenges, and then becomes complete. He is washed in love; the permanent force. He breathes and accepts the end - "as a cycle I shall endure, like a crop..." - but even then he will fight for a fraction of time, just a bit more, to delight in the magic of all and rest assured he has fully understood.

—YARELI ARIZMENDi, *Film Writer, Actress and Director*

The first challenge these poems are faced with is to hold up to the author's autobiographical account of his life. In all honesty I thought this charge was pretentious. But, as I sat down to read, I found that every other line was as if he were speaking about me. I then understood that this autobiography belongs to us. Panagiotis succeeds in making us feel this. The language is clean, direct, and passionate and this, ultimately, is the goal of poetry.

—SERGIO ARAU, *Film Writer and Director*

AN AUTOBIOGRAPHY

ποιήματα

poems

PANAGIOTIS A. TSONIS

DOS MADRES

2016

DOS MADRES PRESS INC.
P.O.Box 294, Loveland, Ohio 45140
www.dosmadres.com   editor@dosmadres.com

Dos Madres is dedicated to the belief that the small press is essential
to the vitality of contemporary literature as a carrier of the new voice,
as well as the older, sometimes forgotten voices of the past. And in an
ever more virtual world, to the creation of fine books pleasing to the
eye and hand.

Dos Madres is named in honor of Vera Murphy and Libbie Hughes,
the "Dos Madres" whose contributions have made this press possible.

Dos Madres Press, Inc. is an Ohio Not For Profit Corporation and a
501 (c) (3) qualified public charity. Contributions are tax deductible.

Executive Editor: Robert J. Murphy

Illustration & Book Design: Elizabeth H. Murphy
www.illusionstudios.net

Typset in Adobe Garamond Pro & Calibri
ISBN 978-1-939929-64-8
Library of Congress Control Number: 2016952590

First Edition

ACKNOWLEDGEMENTS

Translation credits:

From Miguel Hernández: Willis Barntone, 1993
From Octavio Paz: Eliot Weindberger, 1990

Max Heindel's quote is from the Jon Thompson book
"How to read a modern painting," Abrams, New York, 2006

I am grateful to Robert J. Murphy, Executive editor, Dos
Madres Press, for his support and help with the editing of
the manuscript and to Elizabeth H. Murphy for the excel-
lent and meaningful cover and production.

For Katis, my anagram

TABLE OF CONTENTS

I am here with three wounds:
One of life,
One of death,
One of love.

Miguel Hernández, 1939

SUMMARY

My world is audacious
And has no boundaries.
I live
In a lighthouse
Illuminating
Two-dimensional houses
And decomposed landscapes.
I live as a leaf
In a paper tree
That timorously envies
Icarus's fall
Under a dangerous sun
And a full silver moon.
I worship liquid crystals
That tell stories
I live in a painting
Without people
And in another one
With nameless throngs
On a moon walk.
I wander in cities
Never seen before
With fabled storytelling palaces.
I only hear you
As a croon wave
Echoing at fishermen's
Boats no matter
How new
Ancient or true.
I live in your magic

That transforms people
To grand peacocks
And to never-ending
Good-and-evil
Gamblers
Like two rivers
Running opposite to each other
In deep blue colors
One for gain and the other for loss
White and black sails that named oceans.
I live to cherish
Your face
Drawn out with ink lines
That make you be
Primitive and simple
As the clay that built us.

WAITING FOR THE POSTMAN

A letter
Is written to tell
Truths or throes
Because we are out
Of spoken words
So we prefer
That it travels oceans
In a bottle
Than facing the eyes that
Yearn to be seen
So be it, I will write a letter
Rather, a poem to be published
In one of your dreams
With characters borrowed
From astral arrangements
An alphabet that moves
In medieval times
Like a human dragging his feet
In mud-filled streets
Or in modern times
Falling like a colorful parachute
An alphabet that was borrowed
By a foreign species
With the habit of looking at the stars
Messages conveyed with a thought
Like a laugh that unguarded you
An arrangement that never betrays
The observer
You were the observer
And I was the earth

That minded my rain forests and deserts
You became a celestial assemblage
That sent fiery arrows
To immobilize me
Happy now?
The Gods of Greece
Have transformed me
To a sun that can only direct
Its rays to you
What a punishment!
Forever together.

FRAGMENTED BLUE

Blue: limitlessness, a void in which... divine oneness prevails.
Max Heindel, 1911

According to a myth
The sun was once icy blue
And for a reason
That defies any explanation
It started bleeding
And a heart was born
And from within it
The fire.

A different story claims that
The sun's bride
Plucked red flowers
Spring's first
For her crown
From Demeter's forbidden garden
And the furious Goddess
Turned them to blood drops
And thus fire was born.

So, blood fused with light
And mysteriously it
Created day and night
Death and life
Fragmented blue.

THE BLUEPRINT OF LIFE

I will start from scratch. What will be better but pure white
Like the land of the Gate lightened by the May winds
In 1953
First for life
First for height
And color vision.
White canvas, my life
Was blinded by fireworks and lights
In many colors and shapes
But in a corner I noticed
Red, deep red like blood
At my will transforming
To tulips
Bleeding tulips
Changing shapes and colors
Becoming on one hand wings and on another red suns
Creating breaths that feed
Needful mouths
But I drank the red sun
Collecting its tears
On a Peloponnesian hand.

MY BIRTH

Spread out my heart
Spill out your tissues and blood
And let me measure your might
They say you harbor love in
Every poem and that you can
Recite all of them
So, let me know
What you will do tonight
When there is no moon
When volcanos don't erupt
And when beasts guard my sleep
Beasts made up in dreams
Howling in despair
Their bodies touch heaven and earth
Is this the night that will bear
A fiery soul?
Wings ejected from
Uncontrolled rivers?

A PHOTOGRAPH

Bold eyes
Fixed
To eternity
Depicted on a
Golden mask
Of death
(Hephaestus task?)
Old like the winds
That sculpted Olympus.
Decisive
Pursed lips
Wavy hair
Lions' mane
Surrounded by snakes
Spreading fear
Reassuring power
And a hint
Of loneliness.
A prophesy
Delivered
From the serenity
Of your eyes
Like an Oracle promising
A much coveted glory
Even when dead.
Yet, your eyes
Seem like seeds
Ready to transform gold
Into fiery beacons
To guide me home.

FIRST FLIGHT

A leaf on a tree
One of many, maybe thousands, they are all my brothers
How nice to be a leaf on a tree!
You come back every spring, regeneration freak!
And you come back from the same bough
Okay for the moment
But what a boring life
Resurrecting yourself at the same place at the same time
I guess the favorite moment of your (repeated) life is
    when you fall down
A free fall!
A moment you can be free
And explore the little space that becomes available to you.
I never liked paintings depicting flowers and trees
Until I saw this one with paper folds acting as leaves
Some of them were falling under the bright moon
The inconspicuous, the ever wandering, who,
Like leaves, seems to change no residence
It was like they were realizing a dream
They were not afraid of the fall
Even though
It would mean their death
Like Icarus falling out of the sky
Achieving though, momentary flight.

A MAN FOR ALL SEASONS

Snow is falling and its flakes make ugly faces
As they disappear hitting the window that stands between us
Yes, I am protected by this glass
In an infinite bar that has no exit
I hold in my hands a glass of wine
(maybe a projection or continuum of the same glass that is
    protecting me from the snowflakes)
That has the incredible property of recording histories
It reminds me of them by playing them back
A glass-story teller
I look at my glass topped with wine,
A liquid curtain where projected images dance
Images that talk! Images that I converse with
A liquid body that I travelled through
From the Mediterranean Sea
Slipping off to the Atlantic Ocean and then to the Pacific.
I have been at the same bar all over the globe
Funny, when you set to talk to yourself
Time and space don't matter
And the voices around you don't matter
They are just mild winds creating small waves
That clash on the glass walls
Maybe a welcomed aeration that the wine needs
Small waves clashing on rocks
I know because I see them
From my lighthouse
A revolving light illuminating houses in time lapses
Enough darkness to lose a dimension
And the landscapes around them have no coherence
Because between darkness and light

They seem to have no definite body
And make the moon an illusive flame
Like in my dreams that I always prepare for a decisive trip
    that never starts.
I have crossed the oceans and I have seen the same waves
    in (and)
Athens (Prague)
Nagoya (Tokyo)
Beijing (Singapore)
London (Geneva)
Washington D.C. (Seattle)
San Diego (San Francisco)
Milwaukee (Chicago)
Dayton (Cleveland)
Mexico City (Cancun)
Paris (Barcelona)
London (York)
Umea (Stockholm)
Santiago (Cusco)
Montevideo (Buenos Aires)
Sydney (Auckland)
And also in your eyes
Surfacing from the sea
Like two coral jewels.

ATLANTIDES*

Sail to the white bay
That lets you climb icy stairs
Blossomed trees awake.

And welcome you in
Paradise but with a high price
Lost wings up for sale.

Sail to old cities
Protected by a black wall
Use the wings you bought.

A bridge built with flags
Vertical banners take turns
Conquer waves and mist.

Hail to old cities
Whose buildings talk to each other
Glory's upper hand.

Dark city, lost temples
Buried golden statues stand
Reflected in stars.

Unearth them like dreams
Coming true in mind's landscape
Seven white doves fly.

*In Haiku

ALL RIVERS END TO A HEART

Cities of heaven
Cities of dreams
Where you take me
Every night
Riding on a
Flying train
Running on
Perpetual rails
Travelling through
Cities floating on water
With mushroomed trees,
Soaring over circle islands
Houses hanging on the edge
Like crown's golden leaves.
I am walking
On streets
With markets
Desperate people
Running after me
Some of them
I recognize, they look young
But no dimension
And no time
Defines them
Sounds good to me
And my words to them
Are un-finished
Un-deciphered
Endless corridors
Connecting buildings
Transporting me at once
At different places.

...the city that dream us all, that all of us build and unbuild and rebuild as we dream...

Octavio Paz (A tree within, 1976-1987)

ELEFSIS (the coming)

In this deserted city
I find myself in the central square
Covered by countless tiles
Like burned parchments
Every step I take
Liberates the written words
And a sound
Creating a symphony
A mystery.
After several strides
A cave appears calling me
With extending arms
Like a serpent's new skin
They deceive me
Assuring God-given new life.
Blue eyes
Turned black
Betray the sea and the sky
Black eyes
Turned blue
Disorient my feelings.
Half way to hell
Through muddy dark rivers
On a boat steered
By the seeds of Talon,
Half way to spring
Guided by pigments
Escaped from Demeter's crown
Like sparks that

Nourished Demophon.
I know I will take both
A cycle I shall endure
Like a crop's life and death

A SUNRISE FOR ALL SEASONS*

The specter of blue
And red unfolds on summer
Valleys, a deluge.

A secret fret that
Threatens the existence of
The perfect spring love.

The jealous iris
Changes colors selfishly
Fall is always here.

Pale light refuses
To penetrate the old lens
Winter's frozen cloud.

* In Haiku

THE MANY COLORS OF THE MOON

The moonlight
Is the magician of curves
Filling the host
The way ripples
Engage waves
In your case
When an astral pebble
Lean and flat
Sails on your back.
Stubborn light, cosmic printer
Prints only one face
One to keep forever
A pale stone
Never withered
Selene
Serene
Severe
Red, sometimes yellow
Like sulfur
Or white like salt
But never blue
The sky and the sea
Don't cast a shadow on you
Calculated, silenced,
Cold, selfish
Always the same
Eternal wanderer
Arrogant standard of beauty
Adorned by the sunlight,
What would you be without it?

Winter and desert?
Transparent bone
In my chest
A thought of a heart
I worship you
Even when covered by clouds
Epochs of silence
Eternal wanderer
I know your trajectory
So,
I will eventually see you
When the clouds break
Like stones falling
From a cliff
Sharp and white.

But I love you more
During the day
When you compete with the sun
Your face grand and pale
Like an old parchment
Signed by an Emperor
Waving in the blue sky
Like a marionette boat
Engaged in a Greek dance.

Now tell me about the other face of you
The dark,
The one where clouds don't matter
The invisible
Like underground nests

Of worms and rodents
Whose birth
Shuns the essence of your eye's sight
And discovers sunken islands.
You know, dark side
There are two stars
That follow you
Two birds
One real
And the other transparent
Like plastic
Glued together by the wind
Unplanned sparks
Hurled from a burning iron
Like the land that is suddenly born
From a volcano's
Spitting mouth
New land, pure like gems
Gold, sapphire and amethyst.

I can think of you
Distant moon
As a recorder of life
You see everything
The shepherd's need of your guiding light
Or even the cheering
On a boat party
I point my finger at you
And I touch you
It is that simple, we are joined
My finger becomes a needle

That weaves our lives
Mine with a blue thread
I chose this color
Over the red that you like
Because blue lets me navigate
The sea and the sky.

AUTOBIOGRAPHY

Sixty years ago, he took his mother's hand. It was May, his birthday.
....then she wanted him to watch the sun;
they had to stand together as it sank in the possessive earth
Louise Clück, 1985

I am the sun the source of light
I am the living sea aborting trees
On a sandy beach
Made up of thyme and roses
Returning the favor
With beasts transforming
Back to sea life with numerous tentacles.
I am all the blue hues
That make the canvas of the Aegean
Or a handkerchief spilling out of my heart
And I am the tears when a bomb hits it
Blood transformed to dust.
I am the arctic owl at night flying quietly
I am the living crystal with six arms, but never the same
I am the salamander on fire
The sun-loving lizard
I am the blind worm
I am the flying rodent
The bird that changes colors as it sings.
I am this purple flower, no,
I am all the flowers, why so many nice faces!
So, I guess I am the spring I run after
I am the night that doesn't want to end
I am the susurrus the wind creates on wheat lands
I am a flag that never attained one shape
I am the gambler who doesn't deal
I am the pebble sculpted by the intensity of time and waves

I am the lone tree on a rocky cliff
I am the pilot on a plane that is never landing
I am a boat that sails forever
I am a Kabuki dancer, moving with small discreet steps
I am Ai, dripping red tears from white porcelain eyes
I am a drunk Greek dancer
I am a Midwest heart
I am a creature with legs on three continents.
I am two beady eyes, two glassy earths
Revolving in opposite ways
Europe, Asia, America becoming one
I am a torn-apart face looking for a candle, like a fake
opera singer
I am a face with fixed lips; (pursed lips)
I am a bleeding face that attempted to smile
Others would think I am a clown with painted lips
Only that paint doesn't drip…
As I turn against the sunset I am angry
I am cynical and I believe I live in a comedy
I am Sisyphus living my torture over and over
I am all the grotesque faces I created
I am the truths that I created
And the counter-lies.
I am a loner but never acting on a whim
I am an enemy and a lover singing like a child
Holding an amulet praying that his dreams
Will dawn when the moon splashes her wings
Over the light she sheds when she rises over the oceans
Like a flaming needle.
I am a creature of the past
Regenerating its heart because I forget to love

I am the ruins of Athens and Elefsis
I am a church built on clouds
A deserted home that doesn't set the ghost free
I am a brush stroke in paintings; so I belong in all of them
I am a hand that manages to play the piano; a lonely tune
I am all the names
I am Persephone's lover
I am asphodel spreading along the Elysian field
I am the golden rain
Eroding the underground
That keeps you captive
I am Hercules's thirteenth deed
I am Dionysus's disciple.
I am a tear bigger than an eye
Even bigger than a head,
A tilted head, I am a gem
A stone that was carried from Olympia to Parthenon
That built 69 columns
Parallel but bend to a point
Like synchronized lasers focusing to heavens.
I am the thought that runs under the hot sun
Naked
I am burned, my face looks like a map
Oceans and lands joggled in my hands.
I am chased by a bee at midday
She wants to dance, she promises to reveal a story she heard
From poppies that blush as red blood
I am the light this blood becomes when is read
As the Perseids become sudden sparks when colliding
With earth's breath.
I am wings, two wings, four, wings, many wings

Flying in slow motion to reveal
Anything you need
If meteors try to blow apart your heart
I'll hold the dust
From reaching your eyes, precious like old murals.
I am the omnipotent eye
For some my gaze emanates from the bluest
Like the blue on the bottom of a fire
And for others form a hybrid of blue and olive green
Colored eyes of a wild wolf
Torrents, storms that will not let you sleep.
I am all the stories my eyes can tell
I am life in another planet; maybe an ambassador
I am a bleeding star, spurting new life
I am the moon's tailor
I promise simple but elegant shades for which
All the world will talk of.
I am a new dimension; call it fourth or tenth
I am Adam's rib, an immortal medusa.
I endured a fever and I am dressed with woolen clothes
And I play prophesied songs coming out of a poll
My whole being floods out my fingers
Like neurotransmitters
Probably the best day of my life
Majestic, as a soaring eagle
A flag waved by five billion people
Grandiose, as when ten billion hands reach to the heavens
Magnificent as a Christmas song sung to an orphan
Rewarded with an orange.
Alone, hitting the keyboard
Like they are steps making me ascending

A stairway made of billions of pairs
I am the result of this music
Sound transformed in three dimensions
Black and white doves
Fleeing from my head
I am the wind that follows them
I am Aeolus and I have challenged Odysseus
I am just an explosive breath landing on god's palms
Pyrotechnic dust forming new kingdoms and runaway comets.
I am a statue, a soulless one
Holding my head with my hands
Still but thoughtful, reciting histories
In other words,
I am a simple old man, bending over your garden
To pluck a flower to adorn my jacket
Spiral, circular, imposing calligraphy
In mirror symmetry.
And then happily I will sit on a stone
In front of my favorite tree and I will count
For hours and hours, for eons
(nan jikan demo)
All the leaves that fall
Like countless thoughts with the hope
That I am one of them that will return next spring…
Yes is me after all
Written in stones
I am the one language that all derived from
Repetitive and palindromic like an ancient verse
AilihphiliA,
In girum imus nocte et consumimur ignI
(we go wandering at night and are consumed by fire)

The cry of a distant May, 500 years ago
Fearful hands washing the sins not only the face
(Nipson anomemata me monan opsiN
ΝΙΨΟΝΑΝΟΜΗΜΑΤΑΜΗΜΟΝΑΝΟΨΙΝ)
I am history repeating itself, something like a tree branch
Where you can count its leaves both ways
Like them I'll go but I shall be back
Like a palindrome that starts where it ends.
I am the universal verse that creates poems
In other words the center of it all
I created a wind-language to transport my poems
Carried on wings of colored butterflies and birds, thus
I am all the broken wings
Whose dust casts colors on the earth.
I am the shadow that doesn't melt
Doesn't dissolve or dissipates
I am your servant and I will follow you to the end...
I am O.M.N.I.
One Man, Nevertheless Important
Magnus Maior Maximus.
I am the child who yearns to wake up
To play hopscotch 62 times, obviously a dream memory
Jumping softly as caressing a bird's feathers
On the Aegean tableau teasing the waves
Like a cunning animal avoiding traps
Gracefully because it knows of its death,
But not yet.
I obviously have a birthplace
I am the sun after all
I am the emperor
I am the red drop on white flags

Perfectly round balloons filling the sky.
I walk from a named palace
To a named old roof
A palace that I built and a roof I stayed under
Made up of silent stones
Like day and night
A house overlooking a perfectly symmetrical mountain
Like a tea cup you want to drink from
Filled with cherry blossoms.
I am the mist that surrounds my village
Like a soundless ghost trapped in shrouds
The lava that the imposing summit doesn't let go
I am all the walls that don't let you go.
I love your colors, your eternal rice fields
Your half-moon eyes, wide view
Your dark hair, the dark side of the moon
Held by a stick made of refined bone
Colored to match your kimono.
I am Ai
Love buried in a snowstorm or sand dunes
Or transported to another universe
Or scattered in eternal waters
Like pieces of photos become alive out of an animation
When a nipped flower bud gets another chance
To transform to pale white messenger birds
Flaming skin and bones out of my imagination.
Stepping on chrysanthemums with bare feet
I am the perpetual traveler
I am still seeking an unearthed birthplace, the birth of youth
A mighty knight transformed from a glittering golden body.
I created Iris out of rain droplets

And changed her to a reflecting lens
So that the light travels securely in all dimensions
Revealing all; hiding no secrets.
I am the sun. Nothing exists if I don't
The earth, the stars, and of course you
Because you exist when my light illuminates you.

A SINGULARITY (celebration)

When the sun
The sea and the sky
Attained the
Same color
A mix
Of yellow
Orange
And blood
I knew I succeeded
I am the serpent root
That instead of going deep
I design an intricate network of lines
Like a thread
That united Ariadne and Theseus.

SAILS TO KEEP

I have created a palace at the top of a snow-covered mountain
It is a huge palace and is destined to have many rooms
Each one to harbor a story
When a story is read a candle illuminates from one of the
    countless rooms
But I am cunning
At the feet of the mountain I have built a lake and a river
So, when a story is read another light sparks from the lake
    or the river
Make no mistake
There is a reason I created a lake and a river
When the story reflects on the lake it stays and multiplies
When the story reflects on the river it travels, it goes and
    transforms
Like branches of water separate when hitting a rock
I guess I have done all this because I am lonely
And because I want you to see the reflection of my heart,
As when the moonlight marks a fine line of light in the ocean
When sailing at night.
Here is the magic:
When my story lands on the lake I am secure
When my story flows with the river my life is perilous and
    is beautiful
I let the dark waters of my heart
Guided by curved stones and sharp turns and cataracts
Looking like disheveled hair of an unnamed goddess
I try to hold on you to mingle my arms
With your watery hands
We become branches of an imaginary tree, blue and
    transparent

Like when broken crystals falling on peaceful waters
Sail as flat leaves
Like the pursed lips you loved to kiss.

STORY 1: ENDLESS BLUE

His face rests on his hands
Like an immortal
Marble statue
Making a bold statement
His eyes meet
Nobody's
Except the ones
Of his covert love
Of pure white
Like winter's loneliness.
With his hand
He creates waves
That send men
To perilous tasks
Of guarding the empire
At the end of earth
Where the winds
Know no trend.
A ruler, a king
Born by an
Uncertain fire
Carrying the burning
On an icy heart.
Fix your eyes
In the infinite white
And draw your sword.
She dances
In slow motion
In a long white dress
With blue flowers

Adorning her red curls.
She goes
With furtive glances
Crimson tides
She is not yours
And if a tear
Dare escape your eye
The soldiers must not see
Bend the rules
Turn it to crystal
A new jewel to keep
Go to battle!
Conquer
The endless blue
At the union
Of the sky and the sea
Where the sun and the moon
Alternate birth and death
And earn
The perfect flag
She yearns for.

STORY 2: ENDLESS FLAG

I want you
To walk down the street
In your perfectly ironed
Blue and white dress
And I want all eyes
To turn toward you.
I want the moon
That has just arisen
Desire
Your enormous
Bright eyes
That conquered
The sky
And let her wonder
About the perfection
Of two ellipses.
I want your smile
To make the sun
Frown
I want you to walk
With the finesse
Of a flamingo,
I want to see a peacock
Shunning at your sight his
Gaudy wings
And I want you to dance
As a swan
On a perilous trip.
I want to build you up
With marble

And cover you
With a dress
That will become
An emblem.
I want to sing for you
A song
That will become
An anthem
I want to hold you forever
With my phantom arms
And say words
Born in gasps.
I want you
In a hundred years
From now to
Show me your face in tears
And your body
With extended hands
And finally I want
You to become Goddess
Ruler of the Aegean
An enormous aerial statue
Translating the wind's
Direction.

THE STORY OF DANCE

How can you compose
Thousands of songs
With the same simple rhythm?
2, 2, 1,
2, 2, 1, 1
Numbers stand for moves
Steps or hand waves
Shouts, turns
Or desires
Or the last confession.
As you look at the ground
At a buried hope
Or spring's kernel
Earth's core
A dance that defines
The greatest love
The greatest loss
Riches and bitter scold.

A throb wakes me up
And urges me to dance
Every night.
How can you compose
Thousands of songs
With the same simple rhythm?
Replicate your soul?
Portray it in numerous
Abstract paintings that
Mix incredible colors
In new worlds?

Illusion of parallel columns
From a glorious arrangement?
Imitate my psyche
And adjust to the same song
Like a boat rocking
In friendly waves
Responds to wind's mood.
Transform the sounds
Coming out of me
To flames that travel
As shock waves
Hitting my heart
Like blood that keeps it alive.

The mirror vibrates
And spits out images
From long-ago times
But the song is forever sung
No matter present or past
As flowers know
To blossom every spring
Tuned to an exact rhythm.
Time to sort them out
(the images)
My friend, my only friend
Let the music play
And dance my friend,
Make every move
A word that weaves
The fabric of your legend.

And as I dance
The pulses of light
Create waves
That reflect my image
Resembling frames
Broken
In time lapse
One moment I am
And the other I am not.
Like I exist
In different universes
Are you with me?
Fill the gaps
With moves
And shout
Like a fire going out
Not to burn
But to illuminate the path
We assemble
With fiery footsteps.

Beware! Only in the dark
Moves are not seen
Blood is concealed
In a fiery red sea
As when tears fuse
With rain drops.
You are alone
To conduct your grand
And portentous last act
Like a candle's final drop

Dives in slow motion
As tamed hands,
Clipped wings
Rest on the floor
And let red swollen eyes
Scorn the applause,
Let flowers thrown
In excitement turn to stones
Rocky rain
Self-assembling in statues
That at the unending sound of
2, 2, 1
2, 2, 1, 1
Become transparent actors
Exposing your last word,
That is your world
One of the many
Composed by the same rhythm.

THE STORY OF LOVE

The word Love
Is misunderstood
Because is used
Like ingredients
In a churn.
But is only
One spice
One thought
One letter
Hand-written
Over and over again and again
And again.
One tear
That cannot be held back
As you read it.
A flaming breath
That burns thirsty lips
With a fire-born sword.
Love is an angel
Without wings
Who doesn't fly away.
Love is a bottomless inkwell
That sustains writing
Forever.
Love is a calm sea
Nursing fishermen's
Little boats
And not a tide.
Love doesn't migrate
As birds do before

Winter comes.
Love is the first and last
Word of the day,
The bright and dark
Side of every moon,
A sublime poem
Not an onerous puzzle.
Love is a star
That doesn't blink,
Is a heart that misses
No heartbeat.
A mighty cloud
Full of rain and not
A prey of the wind.
Love rises always
From the east
And is red,
Red like ablaze blood
Red like volcano's dress
Red washed out
From lips in flames
That were never kissed.
Love is a Universe
That once born
Only expands
And invents particles and rules
To stay within
The great heart.
And when the day
Will come to die
One single memory

Will again erupt
And triumph
Will reach the heavens
And I guess,
Will create
A new constellation.

TRANSFORMATION (The story of love)

When light
Becomes dark
Souls move.
Your tears
Medusa's snake hair
The many heads
Of Hydra,
The fire
From dragon's breath
Rolling down your face
Like fiery rivers.
Helpless I look at them
As they mark you
With random tracks
And invade your body
And become transparent
Pearls
And cover you
And glow
As thousands of suns,
You!

DIAMOND HEARTS ARE FOREVER
(Another story of love)

Perpetual rain
Falling on
Perpetual fire
Fixes coal in time and space
Like a tear
Quenching the thirst
Of burning lips
Buried in their cracks
Both are wombs of
The unbreakable species
That is born when it reaches
The volcano's mouth
Expelling it as
Transparent hearts
Hiding no secrets.
If you need a heart
I will die giving you mine
An unplanned heartbeat
Your hand holding my hand
Until we die together.

LIGHT

When sunrays break
Through puffy clouds they
Become spiny needles
Needles that sow lives.
My life was a red sun
I spilled out crystal thoughts
Colors from a glass window
Fruits like singing bells
Glimpses from light penetrating
A dense forest
Rainbows of towering wings
Belonging to beasts.
Like a sun I ascend
As a moon you fade out
I want you to discover me
Like an archeologist
Finding fabled mountain-top lost palaces
And rabid lost tribes
Discerned from impossible skulls
With open blue eyes.

AEGEUS'S LEGEND

At 60 I am a well walked stone-spread
Alley
Not much I can offer
Only empty space for autumn leaves to land.

So, when I climb my bed to sleep
After wine and music
I dream of an endless trip
Impregnated with youthful faces
Never-ending
Like the shades of the moon.
I see my vigorous face
Forcefully spilling out of an everlasting glass
Like tears
Bigger than eyes
Bigger than heads
Bigger than suns
Become a deluge
Or black sails
That will tear my body apart
Scattered like leaves
On a free fall.

But I will be back
Because I have patiently
Observed you
And yearned to drink
Drop by drop your youth again.
You have adorned my life
Like a flower opening fast

As in time lapse,
So we will live together
As long as the Aegean Sea
Reflects the blue sky
Like a mind
With blue eyes.

EXCEEDING THE SPEED OF LIGHT
OR THE STORY OF DEATH

When the moment to go will come
I will kneel
On any ground
That will receive me.
And unite
The remaining tears
With every drop in oceans
The last gasp
With every breath that makes
The wind be
The source of rustling
So that in a sense
I will always be touching you
I will recall
Every handshake
Every stealthy glimpse
And smile
That shaped my life
Every ardent heartbeat
Evoked as I yearned
The empty space that will
Somehow
Materialize you
Where our wings entwine again.

Sacred moment!
Extend your life
And let me tame time

To transport back
The monotonous rain
That elicited no effect
And the sudden thunder
That shuttered my soul,
The moves I invented
When I danced
To songs you sang.
I want to tell you
Billions of words
A prattle
Maybe out of nervousness
For I understand
They will be counted
In an instant.

When I go
I hope the ground beneath me
Will be riven
Like a rocky heart
To tell me in the end
Why I bleed
Hear my plea:
Ten more seconds
To bring to mind
When we roamed the world
Riding winged dragons
With gleaming eyes
Fire from a blazing heart
Flames like countless mirrors
Reflecting your face

In tandem repeats
And then
Give me a moment
For the two golden coins' act
To slowly place one of my hands
In my mouth
And the other
To shield my eyes
In disbelief.

A SIMPLE QUESTION ASKED AFTER MY TRIP
TO THE GREAT RIVER
(Anabasis)

Psyche: Goddess, keeper of secrets
That you define the banks of rivers
Where the croaking of frogs
And the jumping fish
Disappear
Like the mist when blown by the winds
What is life?
-Is a stairway to sunlight
When you ascend it
Stars and moons
Will crown you with countless needles
Penetrating your skin
Every day
Blossom your blood
Like cherries.

How important it must be
to someone
that I am alive, and walking,
and I have written
these poems.
This morning the sun stood
right at the end of the road
and waited for me.

Ted Kooser, 2000

NOTES

ELEFSIS P.14

Elefsis (also spelled as Eleusis), a city 20 kilometers (12.5 miles) west of Athens was the site of Eleusian Mysteries offered for the cult of Demeter, dated back to the Mycenean period (c. 1600 – 1100 BC),. Demeter, a goddess disguised as an old woman, arrived at Elefsis in search for her daughter Persephone who was abducted by Pluto. Demeter became the nurse of Demophon, the son of the king of Elefsis. Talon is a mythical beast.

AUTOBIOGRAPHY P.21

"Ai" in Japanese means "love."

"Nan jikan demo" is an expression in Japanese meaning "For whatever time it takes," or "long time."

"In girum imus nocte et consumimur ignI" a palindrome in Latin meaning: "we go wandering at night and are consumed by fire." (source: Wikipedia)

"Nipson anomemata me monan opsiN" in Greek: "NIΨONANOMHMATAMHMONANOΨIN" is a palindrome inscribed on a font outside the church of Hagia Sophia in Constantinople. It means "Wash the sins not only the face." (source: Wikipedia)

THE STORY OF DANCE P.36

2,2,1,2,2,1,1 is the beat of the Greek dance jeibekiko.

ABOUT THE AUTHOR

Born in Greece, PANAGIOTIS A. TSONIS received his primary education and graduated from the University of Patras. Tsonis continued his graduate and post-graduate studies in Japan and in the United States. Tsonis is currently Professor of Molecular Biology at the University of Dayton in Ohio. He has published more than 200 scientific papers and books. He has also co-translated into English the epic book-length poem *Kyra Frossini* by Aristotelis Valaoritis (Nostos Books, 2008). This is his first collection of poetry, strongly influenced by his life and culture in the three counties he has lived.

Author photo by Patricia Steur.

BOOKS BY DOS MADRES PRESS

▷ **2004**
Annie Finch - *Home Birth*
Norman Finkelstein - *An Assembly*
Richard Hague - *Burst, Poems Quickly*
Robert Murphy - *Not For You Alone*
Tyrone Williams - *Futures, Elections*

▷ **2005**
Gerry Grubbs - *Still Life*
James Hogan - *Rue St. Jacques*
Peter O'Leary - *A Mystical Theology of the Limbic Fissure*
David Schloss - *Behind the Eyes*
Henry Weinfield - *The Tears of the Muses*

▷ **2006**
Paul Bray - *Things Past and Things to Come*
Michael Heller - *A Look at the Door with the Hinges Off*
Michael Heller - *Earth and Cave*
Richard Luftig - *Off The Map*
J. Morris - *The Musician, Approaching Sleep*

▷ **2007**
Joseph Donahue - *The Copper Scroll*
Pauletta Hansel - *First Person*
Burt Kimmelman - *There Are Words*
Robert Murphy - *Life in the Ordovician*
William Schickel - *What A Woman*

▷ **2008**
Michael Autrey - *From The Genre Of Silence*
Paul Bray - *Terrible Woods*
Eric Hoffman - *Life At Braintree*
Henry Weinfield - *Without Mythologies*

❯2009

Jon Curley - *New Shadows*
Deborah Diemont - *Wanderer*
Norman Finkelstein - *Scribe*
Nathan Swartzendruber - *Opaque Projectionist*

❯2010

Gerry Grubbs - *Girls in Bright Dresses Dancing*
Michael Henson - *The Tao of Longing & The Body Geographic*
Keith Holyoak - *My Minotaur*
Madeline Tiger - *The Atheist's Prayer*
Donald Wellman - *A North Atlantic Wall*

❯2011

Pauletta Hansel - *What I Did There*
Eric Hoffman - *The American Eye*
David M. Katz - *Claims of Home*
Burt Kimmelman - *The Way We Live*
Bea Opengart - *In The Land*
David A. Petreman - *Candlelight in Quintero-bilingual ed.*
Paul Pines - *Reflections in a Smoking Mirror*
Murray Shugars - *Songs My Mother Never Taught Me*
Madeline Tiger - *From the Viewing Stand*
James Tolan - *Red Walls*
Martin Willetts Jr. - *Secrets No One Must Talk About*
Tyrone Williams - *Adventures of Pi*

❯2012

Jennifer Arin - *Ways We Hold*
Jon Curley - *Angles of Incidents*
Sara Dailey - *Earlier Lives*
Richard Darabaner - *Plaint*
Deborah Diemont - *Diverting Angels*

Richard Hague - *During The Recent Extinctions*
R. Nemo Hill - *When Men Bow Down*
W. Nick Hill - *And We'd Understand Crows Laughing*
Keith Holyoak - *Foreigner*
Pamela L. Laskin - *Plagiarist*
Austin MacRae - *The Organ Builder*
Rick Mullin - *Soutine*
Pam O'Brien - *The Answer To Each Is The Same*
Lianne Spidel & Anne Loveland - *Pairings*
Henry Weinfield - *A Wandering Aramaean*
Donald Wellman - *The Cranberry Island Series*
Anne Whitehouse - *The Refrain*

❯2013

Mary Margaret Alvarado - *Hey Folly*
John Anson - *Jose-Maria de Heredia's Les Trophées*
Gerry Grubbs - *The Hive-a book we read for its honey*
Ruth D. Handel - *Tugboat Warrior*
Eric Hoffman - *By the Hours*
Nancy Kassell - *Text(isles)*
Sherry Kearns - *Deep Kiss*
Owen Lewis - *Sometimes Full of Daylight*
Mario Markus - *Chemical Poems-One For Each Element*
Rick Mullin - *Coelacanth*
Robert Murphy - *From Behind The Blind*
Paul Pines - *New Orleans Variations & Paris Ouroboros*
Murray Shugars - *Snakebit Kudzu*
Jason Shulman - *What does reward bring you but to bind you to Heaven like a slave?*
Olivia Stiffler - *Otherwise, we are safe*
Carole Stone - *Hurt, the Shadow-the Josephine Hopper poems*
Brian Volck - *Flesh Becomes Word*
Kip Zegers - *The Poet of Schools*

▶2014

John Anson - *Time Pieces - poems & translations*
Ann Cefola - *Face Painting in the Dark*
Grace Curtis - *The Shape of a Box*
Dennis Daly - *Nightwalking with Nathaniel-poems of Salem*
Karen George - *Swim Your Way Back*
Ralph La Charity - *Farewellia a la Aralee*
Patricia Monaghan - *Mary-A Life in Verse*
Rick Mullin - *Sonnets on the Voyage of the Beagle*
Fred Muratori - *A Civilization*
Paul Pines - *Fishing on the Pole Star*
Don Schofield - *In Lands Imagination Favors*
Daniel Shapiro - *The Red Handkerchief and other poems*
Maxine Silverman - *Palimpsest*
Lianne Spidel & Anne Loveland - *A Bird in the Hand*
Sarah White - *The Unknowing Muse*

▶2015

Stuart Bartow - *Einstein's Lawn*
Kevin Cutrer - *Lord's Own Anointed*
Richard Hague - *Where Drunk Men Go*
Ruth D. Handel - *No Border is Perennial*
Pauletta Hansel - *Tangle*
Eric Hoffman - *Forms of Life*
Roald Hoffmann - *Something That Belongs To You*
Keith Holyoak - *The Gospel According to Judas*
David M. Katz - *Stanzas on Oz*
Sherry Kearns - *The Magnificence of Ruin*
Marjorie Deiter Keyishian - *Ashes and All*
Jill Kelly Koren - *The Work of the Body*
Owen Lewis - *Best Man*
Rick Mullin - *Stignatz & the User of Vicenza*
Paul Pines - *Message from the Memoirist*

Samantha Reiser - *Tomas Simon and Other Poems*

Quanita Roberson - *Soul Growing-Wisdom for thirteen year old boys from men around the world*

David Schloss - *Reports from Babylon and Beyond*

Eileen R. Tabios - *INVENT[ST]ORY Selected Catalog Poems and New 1996-2015*

Kip Zegers - *The Pond in Room 318*

❧ 2016

Eduardo Chirinos - *Still Life with Flies [naturaleza muerta con moscas]*, Bilingual, English translation by G. J. Racz

Norman Finkelstein - *The Ratio of Reason to Magic: New & Selected Poems*

Gerry Grubbs - *The Palace of Flowers*

R. Nemo Hill - *In No Man's Ear*

W. Nick Hill - *Blue Nocturne*

Nancy Kassell - *Be(longing)*

Rick Mullin - *Stignatz & the User of Vicenza*

Sharon Olinka - *Old Ballerina Club*

Bea Opengart - *Duties of the Heart, a Verse Memoir*

Michael Rothenberg - *Drawing the Shade*

Natalie Safir - *Eyewitness*

Daniel Shapiro - *Woman at the Cusp of Twilight*

Madeline Tiger - *The Clearing*

John J. Trause - *Picture This: For Your Eyes and Ears*

Leonard Trawick - *A 24-Hour Cotillion*

John Tripoulas - *A Soul Inside Each Stone*

Panagiotis A. Tsonis - *An Autobiography*

Anne Whitehouse - *Meteor Shower*

Geoffrey Woolf - *Learn to Love Explosives*

David Almaleck Wolinsky - *The Crane is Flying - Early Poems*

Tyrone Williams - *Between Red & Green: Narrative of the Black Brigade*

www.dosmadres.com